C000139473

Ten War Poems

ex libris

Candlestick Press

Published by:
Candlestick Press,
Diversity House, 72 Nottingham Road, Arnold, Nottingham NG5 6LF, UK
www.candlestickpress.co.uk

Printed by Ratcliff & Roper Print Group, Nottinghamshire, UK

ISBN 978 1 907598 38 8

Acknowledgements:
Our thanks to Andrew Motion for selecting and introducing these
poems, also for permission to print 'The Gardener' from 'Coming
Home', winner of The Poetry Society's Ted Hughes Award for New
Work in Poetry 2014. 'The Gardener' also appears in *Peace Talks*
(Faber & Faber, 2015). Excerpt from *Memorial: A Version of Homer's
Iliad* © 2011 by Alice Oswald is used by permission of W. W. Norton
& Company Inc and Faber & Faber Ltd. Stevie Smith, 'I Remember'
is from *Collected Poems of Stevie Smith,* copyright © 1972 by Stevie
Smith. Reprinted by permission of New Directions Publishing Corp.
and Faber & Faber Ltd. Rihaku/Li Bai, 'Lament of the Frontier Guard'
translated by Ezra Pound is from *Personae* copyright © 1926 by Ezra
Pound and is reprinted by permission of New Directions Publishing
Corp and Faber & Faber Ltd. 'Facing It' by Yusef Komunyakaa is
from *Dien Cai Dau* © 1988 by Yusef Komunyakaa and is reprinted
by permission of Wesleyan University Press. Miroslav Holub, 'The
fly' translated by George Theiner is from *Poems Before and After:
Collected English Translations,* translated by Ian and Jarmila Milner
et al (Bloodaxe Books, 2006).

Donation to Kissing it Better, www.kissingitbetter.co.uk

Where poets are no longer living, their dates are given.

Contents

Introduction

The invitation to compile this anthology of ten war poems came with one condition: that I include my own poem 'The Gardener'. It seemed a price worth paying, for the very interesting challenge of compressing such an enormous, varied and arresting tradition of writing into such a small space. In the end, and withholding strong guilt-feelings about omitting a large number of classic poems that immediately demanded to be included, I decided to settle on poems that might be slightly less familiar than the most famous examples by Wilfred Owen, Siegfried Sassoon, Isaac Rosenberg, Edward Thomas, David Jones, Ivor Gurney and others. I wanted to catch the subject by surprise, and allow us to think about it and imagine it in fresh ways.

Because the fact is: in the UK at least, poetry of the First World War has been fed so deeply into the national consciousness, its terms and conditions have come close to defining the character of all war poetry. That means too little attention has been paid to war poems that deal with things differently – more obliquely, perhaps, or with a closer eye on the civilian experience, or in more broken forms. In the poems that follow, we hear a range of voices from this country and beyond, from ancient history and the present. They all have feelings in common – fear, dread, regret, horror, defiance, sorrow. And they all express them in ways that make us concentrate on the individuality of their authors and their subjects.

Andrew Motion

From **Memorial**

Recently arrived and camping apart from everyone
With weapons cleaned and layed down like cutlery
This is horrible this is some kind of bloodfeast
And beside each man his horses
Twelve anonymous Thracians were killed in their sleep
Before their ghosts had time to keep hold of their names
It was so sudden
The raw meat smell of their bodies woke up the dogs
And these were rich men

They had long smooth hair but Diomedes
Red-faced quietly like a butcher keeping up with his order
Got rid of them
And the last one RHESUS was a king
He should never have come here
Bringing over the water those huge white horses
With their chains and painted cheek guards
Extraordinary creatures almost marble but moving

Like wolves always wanting something
Thin shapes always working the hills
When a shepherd lets his flocks wander
And the weaklings bleat their fear
Within seconds wolves will appear

Alice Oswald

The fly

She sat on a willow-trunk
watching
part of the battle of Crécy,
the shouts,
the gasps,
the groans,
the trampling and the tumbling.

During the fourteenth charge
of the French cavalry
she mated
with a brown-eyed male fly
from Vadincourt.

She rubbed her legs together
as she sat on a disembowelled horse
meditating
on the immortality of flies.

With relief she alighted
on the blue tongue
of the Duke of Clervaux.

When silence settled
and only the whisper of decay
softly circled the bodies

and only
a few arms and legs
still twitched jerkily under the trees,

she began to lay her eggs
on the single eye
of Johann Uhr,
the Royal Armourer.

And thus it was
that she was eaten by a swift
fleeing
from the fires of Estrées.

Miroslav Holub (1923 – 1998)

The Artilleryman's Vision

While my wife at my side lies slumbering, and the wars are
    over long,
And my head on the pillow rests at home, and the vacant
    midnight passes,
And through the stillness, through the dark, I hear, just hear,
    the breath of my infant,
There in the room as I wake from sleep this vision presses
    upon me;
The engagement opens there and then in fantasy unreal,
The skirmishers begin, they crawl cautiously ahead, I hear the
    irregular snap! snap!
I hear the sounds of the different missiles, the short *t-h-t!*
    t-h-t! of the rifle-balls,
I see the shells exploding leaving small white clouds, I hear the
    great shells shrieking as they pass,
The grape like the hum and whirr of wind through the trees,
    (tumultuous now the contest rages,)
All the scenes at the batteries rise in detail before me again,
The crashing and smoking, the pride of the men in their pieces,
The chief-gunner ranges and sights his piece and selects a fuse
    of the right time,
After firing I see him lean aside and look eagerly off to note
    the effect;
Elsewhere I hear the cry of a regiment charging, (the young
    colonel leads himself this time with brandish'd sword,)
I see the gaps cut by the enemy's volleys, (quickly fill'd up, no
    delay,)
I breathe the suffocating smoke, then the flat clouds hover low
    concealing all;
Now a strange lull for a few seconds, not a shot fired on either
    side,
Then resumed the chaos louder than ever, with eager calls and
    orders of officers,

While from some distant part of the field the wind wafts to my
ears a shout of applause, (some special success,)
And ever the sound of the cannon far or near, (rousing even in
dreams a devilish exultation and all the old mad joy in the
depths of my soul,)
And ever the hastening of infantry shifting positions, batteries,
cavalry, moving hither and thither,
(The falling, dying, I heed not, the wounded dripping and red I
heed not, some to the rear are hobbling,)
Grime, heat, rush, aide-de-camps galloping by or on a full run,
With the patter of small arms, the warning *s-s-t* of the rifles,
(these in my vision I hear or see,)
And bombs bursting in air, and at night the vari-color'd
rockets.

Walt Whitman (1819 – 1892)

The Send-Off

Down the close, darkening lanes they sang their way
To the siding-shed,
And lined the train with faces grimly gay.

Their breasts were stuck all white with wreath and spray
As men's are, dead.

Dull porters watched them, and a casual tramp
Stood staring hard,
Sorry to miss them from the upland camp.
Then, unmoved, signals nodded, and a lamp
Winked to the guard.

So secretly, like wrongs hushed-up, they went.
They were not ours:
We never heard to which front these were sent.

Nor there if they yet mock what women meant
Who gave them flowers.

Shall they return to beatings of great bells
In wild train-loads?
A few, a few, too few for drums and yells,
May creep back, silent, to still village wells
Up half-known roads.

Wilfred Owen (1893 – 1918)

Lament of the Frontier Guard

translated from the Chinese by Ezra Pound

By the North Gate, the wind blows full of sand,
Lonely from the beginning of time until now!
Trees fall, the grass goes yellow with autumn.
I climb the towers and towers
      to watch out the barbarous land:
Desolate castle, the sky, the wide desert.
There is no wall left to this village.
Bones white with a thousand frosts,
High heaps, covered with trees and grass;
Who brought this to pass?
Who has brought the flaming imperial anger?

Who has brought the army with drums and with kettle-drums?
Barbarous kings.
A gracious spring, turned to blood-ravenous autumn,
A turmoil of wars-men, spread over the middle kingdom,
Three hundred and sixty thousand,
And sorrow, sorrow like rain.
Sorrow to go, and sorrow, sorrow returning.
Desolate, desolate fields,
And no children of warfare upon them,
      No longer the men for offence and defence.
Ah, how shall you know the dreary sorrow at the North Gate,
With Rihaku's name forgotten,
And we guardsmen fed to the tigers.

Li Bai (705 – 762) also known as Rihaku

That Shit Shute

(Air: 'Wrap Me Up in My Tarpaulin Jacket')

The General inspecting the trenches
Exclaimed with a horrified shout,
'I refuse to command a Division
Which leaves its excreta about.'

But nobody took any notice
No one was prepared to refute,
That the presence of shit was congenial
Compared with the presence of Shute.

And certain responsible critics
Made haste to reply to his words
Observing that his Staff advisers
Consisted entirely of turds.

For shit may be shot at odd corners
And paper supplied there to suit,
But a shit would be shot without mourners
If somebody shot that shit Shute.

Anonymous

Vergissmeinnicht

Three weeks gone and the combatants gone
returning over the nightmare ground
we found the place again, and found
the soldier sprawling in the sun.

The frowning barrel of his gun
overshadowing. As we came on
that day, he hit my tank with one
like the entry of a demon.

Look. Here in the gunpit spoil
the dishonoured picture of his girl
who has put: *Steffi. Vergissmeinnicht*
in a copybook gothic script.

We see him almost with content,
abased, and seeming to have paid
and mocked at by his own equipment
that's hard and good when he's decayed.

But she would weep to see today
how on his skin the swat flies move;
the dust upon the paper eye
and the burst stomach like a cave.

For here the lover and killer are mingled
who had one body and one heart.
And death who had the soldier singled
has done the lover mortal hurt.

Keith Douglas (1920 – 1944)

I Remember

It was my bridal night I remember,
An old man of seventy-three
I lay with my young bride in my arms,
A girl with t.b.
It was wartime, and overhead
The Germans were making a particularly heavy raid on
    Hampstead.
What rendered the confusion worse, perversely
Our bombers had chosen that moment to set out for Germany.
Harry, do they ever collide?
I do not think it has ever happened,
Oh my bride, my bride.

Stevie Smith (1902 – 1971)

Facing It

My black face fades,
hiding inside black granite.
I said I wouldn't
dammit: No tears.
I'm stone. I'm flesh.
My clouded reflection eyes me
like a bird of prey, the profile of night
slanted against morning. I turn
this way – the stone lets me go.
I turn that way – I'm inside
the Vietnam Veterans Memorial
again, depending on the light
to make a difference.
I go down the 58,022 names,
half-expecting to find
my own in letters like smoke.
I touch the name Andrew Johnson;
I see the booby trap's white flash.
Names shimmer on a woman's blouse
but when she walks away
the names stay on the wall.
Brushstrokes flash, a red bird's
wings cutting across my stare.
The sky. A plane in the sky.
A white vet's image floats
closer to me, then his pale eyes
look through mine. I'm a window.
He's lost his right arm
inside the stone. In the black mirror
a woman's trying to erase names:
No, she's brushing a boy's hair.

Yusef Komunyakaa

The Gardener

In Memory of Lieutenant Mark Evison

W e spent
many hours kneeling together in the garden
    so many hours
        Mark
he liked lending a hand

watching Gardener's World

building compost heaps

or the brick path with the cherry tree
that grows over it now   the white cherry
    where I thought   I mustn't cry
I must behave
    as if he's coming back

*

It was just after Easter
with everything in leaf

      he is so sweet really
          though worldly
            before his time

I kissed him and said
          See you
in six months   and he turned

    he turned and said

*

I opened the garden for the first time

the National Gardens Scheme
        you know
                what gardens are like in May

and this man was hovering around
        outside the front

as we walked down the side passage
        he said
                I'm a Major

I said   Oh my son   he's in the army
        sort of brightly

*

Then no-one was there

so I went
        and I gardened all day

how slow   how satisfying

I felt next morning
        he was struggling for his life

*

He would be home
        with three transfers
                on three different planes

and if he died they would ring me
        and they would go back
                and they would not keep coming

my daughter Elizabeth and I drove to Birmingham
my mobile   there   on the dashboard

we had worked out the times of the last plane
and we arrived
        and they still hadn't called me
                and he was still

*

He was lying   he was
with this
        Mark
with this big plastic hole
        sort of
a bandage over a hole
        just like
asleep

*

The reindeer   the wild reindeer
        giving birth in the snow
                with the rest of the herd scarpering

they have seen the eagle above them

but the mother stands still
        what am I going to do   what

a bit restless   and everything
        but starting to lick her baby
with the eagle   watching

*

Quietened   that is the best word
to describe it   I felt quietened
seeing the hills below
        as we came into Kabul

I was thinking

                Mark lived in a very green place
and here everything is purple
        orange   Turner colours I call them

in my nightmares he is never dead
bandaged   lost   never dead
with my love
        circling
        nowhere to go

I was thinking

        thousands of lives
              in an instant
and the molecules starting again
   and the mountains never changing

how was I
   quietened
        how

but for a moment
   I was
then losing height
   with the brown earth rushing to meet me.

Andrew Motion